BILL AT RAINBOW BRIDGE

Written for the Owners of Departed Pets

By Dan Carrison

Illustrations by Peg DuVal

Modern Family Classics Publishing
SANTA CLARITA, CA

Copyright © 2010, Dan Carrison

All rights reserved. No part of this book may be used or reproduced in any manner whatsoever without the written permission of the Publisher and Author.

For information visit:

www.BillAtRainbowBridge.com

ISBN 0-9845-6820-4

Illustrations and book design by Peg DuVal, Lafayette, LA

Library of Congress Cataloging-in-Publication Data:

Bill at Rainbow Bridge/Dan Carrison

       [1st Ed.]

       ISBN 0-9845-6820-4

Modern Family Classics Publishing, Santa Clarita, CA

Manufactured in the USA.

FIRST EDITION

To Beverly Berwald —

who, once upon a time as my editor,

gave me the freedom to write like this.

Chapter One

When Bill the Bulldog first arrived at Rainbow Bridge, he couldn't believe his eyes. For one thing, the cloudiness that had plagued his sight later in life had vanished; it seemed as if he could see forever.

And for another, this was a dog park like no other!

Green grass spread out as far as even his newly cleared eyes could see. The sun was a bright yellow in a perfectly blue sky dotted with puffy white clouds. Even so, there was a beautiful rainbow off in one corner of the park, which seemed to cast a veil of dazzling color over the far end of a footbridge.

But things were much more interesting in Bill's immediate

vicinity. There were dogs running around everywhere — and even cats! Colorful birds fluttered through the trees, chirping to each other. And there were no people. No one holding a leash, about to impatiently whistle an end to playtime. Bill had never seen so many dogs at one time — big and small, furry and short-haired, grey-whiskered and young — wagging their tails and yapping with joy as they chased each other and tumbled in the grass.

Nearby, two terriers who could have been brother and sister were playing tug of war with a piece of rope, growling like little tigers, their shining eyes full of merriment. A Golden Retriever dashed into a pond of sparkling water, proudly returning to the shore with a branch in his mouth, as if he were showing the group of onlookers how to do it. To Bill's right, an intrepid black and white kitten slipped off the belly of a large, snoring Labrador. Staring up with renewed determination, the kitten promptly began its climb back up the smooth black mountain.

Bill could see at a glance that some of the dogs bore scars that told of very hard lives. He had seen dogs like this before, snarling behind strong fences or wandering alone and friendless. They would have looked mean and menacing anywhere else; but here

Zack greets Bill at Rainbow Bridge.

they romped like puppies, scampering with playmates half their size that were completely unafraid of them.

A miniature Schnauzer with a mischievous twinkle in his eyes suddenly rushed up to Bill and stared into his serio-comic Bulldog face. Completely unafraid of Bill's size and aspect, the little dog made a series of charging movements, braking with his front paws, and barking an invitation to play. From habit, Bill sadly turned away; he had learned his limitations these last few years. He knew there was no way his old achy body could keep up with the bundle of energy confronting him; why, the little dog was half his age!

But the Schnauzer persisted, with that merry sparkle in his eyes, as if he knew a secret Bill was about to discover. When Bill made a half-hearted attempt to fend off the little prankster, he found to his surprise that he had moved quickly and without pain. He had, in fact, actually spun in a half circle, landing on four firm paws — ready for action. His muscles felt powerful, as if he were young again. Instinctively, Bill lowered himself into the famous Bulldog crouch, and gathered his strength in preparation for a lunge. One bottom tooth protruded over his upper lip; his stubby tail began to wag.

The Schnauzer's laughing eyes regarded Bill's massive shoulders and pugnacious face. Leaping forward, he gave the newcomer a friendly nip on the jowls, and then ran for his life. Bill roared a deep-throated Bulldog response and charged.

The chase was on!

The Schnauzer, whose name was Zack, moved like lightning. With Bill on his tail, he cut to the right and to the left, just out of reach. Bill pursued in Bulldog fashion, his two rear legs driving forward simultaneously, frog-like, while his two forelegs reached out together to take up the advancing earth. While he knew he couldn't outrun the light and speedy Schnauzer, he might be able to outsmart him: the little dog's zigs and zags had become predictable.

Suddenly, Zack zagged into an avalanche of muscle, as both dogs tumbled over each other in a yapping tumult of victory and mock surrender. Bill's huge paws held the squirming Zack as he licked his face. But Zack didn't mind; it was as if they had known each other all their lives.

Soon other dogs rushed over to meet the newcomer. There

was Max, a brown and white Water Spaniel who had been the comedian of the family he had loved; and Linda — a Beagle and Toy Collie mix once famous for her forays into her surrounding neighborhood. A female Pug named Willow, had rushed over at the sight of such a handsome Bulldog as Bill. The smallest visitor, but by no means the most timid, was Chi Chi, a Chihuahua with a heart as big as a St. Bernard's.

Rex, a former police dog who had been awarded the Medal of Valor, introduced himself to Bill by way of a playful nip on the butt. Bill spun around with dancing eyes and faced the taller Shepherd. It was a classic match-up: the tall, strong Shepherd and the squat, powerful English Bulldog. Rex barked a challenge and wagged his tail. Bill roared with joy and charged. The two dogs went at it like two gleeful champions, tumbling over each other and yelping spontaneous cries of happiness. Each seemed to find in the other the perfect test of strength.

Just as the mock fight was about to end in an eternal tie, Zack, Max, Linda, Willow and Chi Chi leapt onto the wrestling duo, each barking in delight. The big ball of dogs rolled down a gentle grassy slope in a mass of wagging tails, slurping lips, and growls of happiness.

And this was how the days passed at Rainbow Bridge. Surrounded by eager playmates, Bill made new friends at every turn.

Since there was no sense of fatigue and no real nighttime at the park — only a wonderful, calming twilight — there was no real reason to sleep. But Bill noticed that most of his playmates took naps anyway. He would watch his friends wander off a short space, each in his-or-her own time, and sprawl beneath the shade of a tree. He knew that Zack, Max, Linda, Willow, Chi Chi and Rex were dreaming by their movements and by their contented sighs; and he knew intuitively that it would have been improper to awaken them in their reveries.

Bill also found it pleasant to lie beneath a shady tree and dream. His playmates showed him the same courtesy, and allowed him to nap, although they did look at each other in amusement as Bill snored. Very few dogs at Rainbow Bridge could match the Bulldog's snoring for volume and pitch.

Bill's dreams were always happy and generally revolved around the playful contests at Rainbow Bridge. But occasionally welcome memories would come into his dreams, and his heart would glow. He would see his friend — a tall man who smiled down on him while balancing a soccer ball in his hand. "Excuse me, Sir," the man would ask, "is this your ball?"

In his sleep, Bill imagined himself in the Bulldog crouch, eyes alternately on the ball and on the man's face, barking in an ecstasy of anticipation.

"Well, go get it, then," the man would laugh, as he hurled the ball away from Bill.

With a cry of delight, Bill would race after the rolling ball until, with a final lunge, he would pounce on it, and grip it between his mighty forepaws. Rarely did a ball pop out of Bill's powerful grip.

The man would call out, "Bring the ball, Bill," and beam with obvious pride as Bill raced back, almost as quickly as he had raced forward, pushing the ball ahead of him with his massive right shoulder. Bill didn't think there was anything unusual about his ability to push a ball down field, but evidently everybody else did: people passing by never failed to stop and stare, with incredulous smiles on their faces, as Bill controlled the ball like a soccer player. Indeed, there were often soccer players in the park, who would come over and talk to the tall man, while admiring Bill. But Bill had eyes only for his friend, whom he loved more than life itself.

Bill enjoyed his naps because he was visited by such wonderful memories. He whimpered with pleasure as he recalled in his dreams how his friend would wrestle with him, and sneak treats down to him from the dinner table, and sing softly into his ear at sleep time. But upon awakening, Bill's memories slipped back where they belonged, and he was emotionally free to join in the general frolic at Rainbow Bridge, where pets ruled!

Chapter Two

F AR AWAY, in another park, where his Bulldog used to amaze onlookers with his ability to control a soccer ball, David Jackson sipped a cup of coffee. Even though Bill had died, David maintained their morning ritual. This was where he and Bill had played nearly every day for ten years. It was a real question as to who enjoyed those sessions more. While Bill was clearly having the time of his life retrieving the soccer ball, David's heart never failed to turn over at the sight of Bill in a Bulldog crouch, his comical face so utterly transparent with joy. When Bill ran after the ball, always at full speed, it had never, in ten years, failed to buoy David's spirit. Just to witness such unabashed pleasure, such spontaneous innocent happiness, had been an on-going privilege and a source of delight. It didn't seem possible that a being so alive, and so radiant with joy, could ever grow old, and could ever die.

David's gaze followed the lines of the park typically traversed by Bill. The park seemed empty and diminished without his presence, as if the spirit of the place had died with him.

He heard the car door open and the sympathetic voice of his wife. "Honey, we've got to go now."

Susan Jackson was frankly worried about her husband. It had been six weeks since Bill had died, yet David continued to mope around the park. He hadn't been able to "get over it" as she had. She had loved Bill, too, but as a dog. David, she knew, had loved Bill as a person — and she had never been able to understand, nor to wholly condone, that kind of love for an animal. It was all very well to acknowledge dogs, in general, as Man's Best Friend, but Bill had literally been her husband's closest buddy.

David had been "best friends" with a dog — not with a human being.

"What," she wondered, "did it say about someone who could relate to a dog on a deeper level than with fellow human beings?"

David, alone, where he and Bill used to play.

Bill had been a great dog, she admitted, but a dog nonetheless. And she didn't think it natural, or even proper, to mourn the loss of an animal with the same intensity one would mourn the passing of a human being. To her way of thinking, David's emotional suffering seemed misplaced — and very nearly an affront to her own grief at the loss of her mother. She had even wondered, at times, if her husband would lament her own passing with the same depth of feeling.

For his part, David sensed that he may be overreacting. His rational mind recognized that all dogs are comparatively short-lived — and especially Bulldogs. Bill, in fact, had done rather well for a big 70 pound English Bulldog. Most big males do not make it past eight years; and Bill had been part of his life for over a decade. David knew he should be grateful for the statistical two year "bonus" of Bill's companionship; instead he was overwhelmed with grief — and felt at times like an unappreciative child.

And it was that sense of embarrassment which made it difficult for him to talk about the effect of Bill's passing. He felt an instinctive, manly sense of shame for being so vulnerable, and so unable to control his emotions since Bill's death. Other people of his acquaintance had lost their dogs to disease or to old age, and they hadn't fallen apart. They had acted like adults. But there seemed nothing he could do about it. The absence of his best friend continued to take his breath away.

The grief came in waves. At one moment he would gain some kind of perspective on the natural course of things, and be able to understand why Bill had left him. But, in another moment, the memory of Bill's Churchillian face looking up at him, man-to-man — like a trusty sidekick on life's journey — would just break his heart. The thought of never seeing that unique being again was unbearable. Bill had been a "bundle of joy" in the truest sense of the expression: he had been Joy incarnate. Now, it just didn't seem conceivable to David that he would ever again experience personal happiness with the intensity made possible by Bill's companionship.

"David?" His wife's voice clearly sounded concerned.

He made an effort to rouse himself, and to pretend he had come to the park for a breath of fresh air. He stretched, commented on the beautiful weather, kissed his wife and got into the car.

That night, over a dinner that he only picked at with his fork, David's wife suggested he seek professional help.

He raised his eyebrows. "You mean, you think I should see a shrink?"

"No: a counselor; a grief counselor — someone who specializes in...pet loss," she finished gently. "A very nice lady at the Humane Society gave me the name of Greg Baxter; they know him well because he's very active in animal rescue."

Susan gave her most persuasive smile. "If you didn't like it, you could just chalk it up to experience. But just try one visit. It would be like talking to a friend — a friend that has had experience in dealing with these problems."

David looked down at his plate. The dinner, he realized, was his favorite dish: a French peasant stew recipe that he knew had required a lot of work in the kitchen. Susan had been trying to please him, and he hadn't even noticed the meal; he had hardly touched it. Glancing up at the patient, loving woman across the table, he acquiesced.

"OK. If you think it would help, I'll go," he said.

Chapter Three

Not long after he arrived at Rainbow Bridge, Bill witnessed something wonderful.

He had been romping with his favorite playmate, Zack. They had been scampering through the park when Zack suddenly stopped in his tracks and cocked his head. He was looking toward the far corner of the park where the bridge merged with the ever present rainbow. Panting from the pleasant exertion, Bill looked too, but saw nothing unusual.

Now Zack cocked his head the other way, totally alert. It seemed as if he had forgotten Bill and everything else. Off in the corner of the park where the rainbow burned brightly, a human figure appeared, silhouetted on top of the grassy hill leading down to the footbridge.

Zack whimpered with curiosity. Suddenly he cried out with joy and ran as fast as his swift legs would carry him toward the footbridge.

Bill felt a reluctance to follow — just as he somehow knew that to wake a napping dog would have been improper. But Zack was his best friend at the park, so he did follow at a respectful distance.

Zack sped toward the footbridge. His high-pitched barks had never sounded so utterly happy to Bill, even at Rainbow Bridge, where all the pets were always happy. At the threshold of the footbridge, Zack screeched to a halt and waited, his pink tongue hanging out. He could hardly contain himself. He squirmed and whimpered with pleasure. Bill had never seen such joy in the little Schnauzer — and that was something, because Zack was always joyful.

This, Bill realized, was something more, something greater.

The human was quite close now — a radiant woman! At the sight of her, Zack went into a perfect rapture of joy as he rose on his hind legs, Schnauzer-style, batting the air with his forepaws, his eyes dancing with recognition. The woman, with one look, fell to her knees and cried out, "Zack!"

As Zack leapt into her arms Bill felt a sudden tug in his heart.

Zack was absolutely beside himself with happiness, as his friend murmured into his ear, and kissed his face over and over again. She clasped Zack to her breast and rocked back and forth shedding tears of gratitude, as he yelped for joy.

Then Zack broke away and pranced out onto the middle of the footbridge, turning back towards the woman. Bill was surprised to see his little playmate stand so confidently on the footbridge — an area where they had never, by common consent, played. But now Zack seemed to know exactly what to do, as he beckoned with joyous barks for the woman to follow. Bemused, as if in a kind of trance, the woman did follow; and the two began to walk across the bridge together — she looking with wonderment left and right, and Zack confidently leading the way, barking and prancing across the bridge.

His heart full, Bill watched the two disappear into the colors of the rainbow at the end of the bridge. It was wonderful to see his little playmate so happy. And he didn't feel as if Zack had left him; somehow he knew that one day they would romp and race, together again.

Like all Bulldogs, Bill was a deep thinker. His furrowed brows contracted even deeper as he lay down in the grass and pondered the scene he had just witnessed.

And, after a while, his little stubby tail began to wag.

Chapter Four

DAVID ENTERED the small waiting room to Greg Baxter's office, half expecting to find it full of anxious clients. He was relieved to see it empty. There wasn't even a receptionist he would have had to put on a hearty show for. The entrance door, he realized, must have sounded a buzzer inside the closed office, for in a moment the inner door opened revealing a robust, grey-haired, white-bearded man in an Aloha shirt.

David smiled wryly to himself as he entered the inner office. He realized he had been slightly disappointed to have been greeted by a mental health professional wearing an Aloha shirt, as if the experience of the office visit had been subtly devalued — as if "getting his money's worth" meant meeting with a serious professional in a suit. Silently, he laughed at his own preconceptions.

Greg Baxter introduced himself in a booming voice, gave him a strong handshake and motioned to an old, battered but very comfortable-looking leather chair. "Have a seat, David."

As David plunged into the deep, beaten leather, his eyes took in the certificates on the wall and the general appearance of the office. He had read somewhere that many doctor's offices have aquariums to relax the patients; this one had, instead, old comfortable furniture, a collection of ancient looking briar pipes, and a counselor who looked like Santa Claus on Hawaiian holiday.

Baxter began the conversation with the usual pleasantries, gradually leading David up to the reason for his visit.

"Well, my wife suggested I speak to someone," he explained.

"Good. Talking always helps. What seems to be the trouble?"

David flushed with embarrassment. So many desperate people must have sat in this same chair, he reflected, with real adult problems; how could he say that his unhappiness was due to his dog dying?

"Well, you see…it's that my Bulldog — Bill was his name — died a short time ago. And I guess I'm overreacting."

"How so?"

"Oh, you know; I don't eat well, can't sleep; I'm distracted at work. I've even," he forced himself to say to this broad, strong-looking older man, "cried out loud. Several times, in fact," he concluded in an almost inaudible afterthought.

"But why," asked the counselor reasonably, "do you consider that to be overreacting?"

David looked up, surprised. "Well, isn't it? I'm sure my wife thinks so. And the guys I know at work — some of them have had dogs die and don't mope around like a child."

Greg Baxter reached forward and grabbed a stubby, ancient pipe out of the rack. "OK if I smoke?" he asked.

"Sure."

"You're positive? You're not just saying that to be polite? Because I don't have to smoke this thing."

David could see by the man's expression that he clearly didn't mean what he said. "Please go ahead; I like the smell of pipe tobacco."

"Ah! Thank you," the older man replied with obvious relish. "It helps me think." He retrieved an old, faded leather pouch from a drawer and soon clouds of aromatic smoke floated to the ceiling. He sighed with contentment. "The fact that some of your coworkers didn't feel as deeply about losing their own dogs," he explained, "could be because they simply didn't love them as deeply as you did yours. Now...tell me about Bill."

David regarded the counselor thoughtfully for several moments, and then appeared to come to a decision. "I believe in getting my money's worth," he said. "And the only way I'm going to benefit from this visit with you is to be perfectly frank. Is that about right?"

Greg Baxter nodded his head approvingly.

"OK. Then I suppose I should describe Bill as my best friend, because that's what he was. He lit up my life with joy. I couldn't wait to get home from work to be with him, roughhouse with him, and take him out to the park. We'd play until his tongue was beginning to hang out; then I'd know he'd had enough. And I'd say 'You're out of gas, Bill.' That was my signal for stopping, and he understood it. Without protest, he would leave his ball where it laid and head for the car, panting like a war horse.

"At night, when it was Bill's bedtime, he would stand before me, solid as a rock, as I sat in my big armchair. If I didn't move he would continue to stare at me with those earnest eyes of his. That was his signal for me to get out of the chair, which was, in fact, his favorite place to sleep the night away. If I didn't get the message, he would bark impatiently. So, of course, I would get up out of the chair and he would immediately leap into it, and settle himself for sleep.

David cleared his throat and took a deep breath. "OK, now I'll tell you the end of my daily routine with Bill, and you'll think I'm over the top. As Bill lay there with his chin on the arm of the chair, falling asleep, I would kneel down and sing softly into his ear. I sang to him every night for ten years — the same stanza every night — and he would just sigh with contentment and fall asleep. Now if that doesn't make me a nut case, nothing does," he concluded with a note of defiance in his voice.

Baxter took the pipe out of his mouth, and asked "What were the words to the song?"

"Oh, just a silly, baby-talk song, like something you would sing to a little child."

"I'm not asking you to sing it, but can you tell me the words?"

"It's silly; you don't want to hear it."

"But I do. Please. It'll help you," he grinned, "get your money's worth out of me."

David averted his eyes and swallowed. "Well, alright…here are the words:

Go to sleep, little Bill

Go to sleep my William,

Count your sheep

As you sleep

Go to sleep dear Bill.

"Like I said, it was a silly, little ditty. But I enjoyed whispering that song into his ear every night. Then…about six weeks ago, I came downstairs in the morning and found that Bill had passed away in that big chair of his. So I knelt down and softly sang that song into his ear...to help send him on his way."

David took a deep breath. "We have a backyard," he continued, "with a nice view of the mountains. It faces west, so we see the sun set every evening. This backyard was, of course, Bill's domain; he often sprawled out on the lawn to take a nap in the sun.

"So, I wrapped Bill up in his soft blanket and went outside and dug a deep grave, out by the fence overlooking the view, and laid Bill into it. It was heart-wrenching. Then I went down to the garden supply place and bought a large bird bath — a wide, stone basin that sets on top of a thick, squat Corinthian pillar. I bought it, you see, because it was built like Bill, strong and steady. Anyway, the birds love it. And I sit out there in the evenings sometimes and talk to Bill."

David's lips tightened with a masculine reluctance to cry in front of another man. But Greg Baxter immediately took the pressure off of him by going into a monologue of his own. It was a great relief to David to hear him talk.

"Most people would say 'My dog died.' You say, instead, that Bill 'passed away.' You're a man after my own heart, David.

"I went through this, myself — only, with me, it was a cat."

Greg Baxter turned the desk photo of a beautiful, confident-looking Tabby toward David. "Fifteen years ago, as I parked on the street in front of my bank, something moved in the curb — and I was a little startled, thinking it might be a rat. But, lying down there in the gutter was a bedraggled kitten. I bent down and took a closer look. Its eyes were mostly shut, encrusted with dirt and sand; the fur was matted and filthy. It moved its head up in my direction, and mewed. I'd never seen anything so utterly helpless."

Refilling his pipe, the older man shrugged. "What could I do? I couldn't just walk away. So, I took out an old sweatshirt from my trunk and picked the little thing up. When I brought it home, my wife took one look and all of her maternal instincts took over. She gave it a bath and we discovered that it was a female. We set a dish of warm milk in front of her and, after much coaxing, she lapped it all up. To make a long story short, the little lady adopted us. We named her Annie, after the sassy, homeless woman Apple Annie in 'A Pocketful of Miracles.'

"Annie recovered, got strong, and revealed herself to be such a character! She was always peeking into drawers, or burrowing under a pillow, or lying in wait like a tiger — and ambushing us, as we walked by, with her soft paws. Annie loved to be stroked and petted, and she expected it of every visitor. I liked to have her here in the office because she had a tranquilizing effect on my clients. There's nothing like a cat purring on the lap," he grinned, "to relieve anxiety. But, of course, I had to share Annie with my wife, who wanted her around the house. At night, when we were home together as a family, Annie seemed to consciously make it a point to spend 'quality time' on both of our laps — as if she were placating us."

David smiled in appreciation of the narrative. "Is Annie still with you?"

"No, Dave. She, too, passed away about a year ago. Feline leukemia. I don't mind telling you that my wife and I hugged each other and cried our eyes out. It took months for me to gain some kind of philosophical perspective; and I think I finally did. No great wisdom. It was only this: that I was the luckiest guy in the world to have parked in that particular spot in front of my bank, on that particular day, at that particular time."

David felt an affinity for this fellow traveler facing him from across the desk. He wanted desperately to agree with Greg, to say, in support of his experience with Annie, that he, too, had reached a similar philosophical perspective with regard to Bill.

But he hadn't; he was still devastated by Bill's death. "I'll be happy — happier — when I can say the same," he said. "But right now, I'm just heartbroken and embarrassed for feeling this way."

"Embarrassed? Why?"

David considered the question with a thoughtful frown. "Not because I'm too macho to cry over Bill. It's not that. I've never been one to try to hide my emotions — although my wife thinks I do. But I think I'm pretty open. So that's not why I'm embarrassed.

"I'm embarrassed," he explained, "because I knew all along this would happen one day, and I feel as if I should have been adult enough to deal with it. I know dogs can't live forever. I knew what I was getting into when I took Bill home as a puppy. I knew he would eventually grow old and die. Nevertheless, I feel like a child who has lost his best friend — and that's what embarrasses me; it's irrational and selfish, but I can't help it."

"Does that mean you'll be embarrassed at your grief if your wife dies before you?" asked the counselor through an extra large puff of tobacco smoke. "After all, you married her knowing she was mortal — and knowing full well that one of you will likely pass away before the other. Was your marriage also an irrational decision?"

David shrugged, as if he were physically deflecting the thrust of Greg's logic, "It's different with people."

"I wonder if it really is." The older man stood and reached into his bookcase for a slim volume. "Don't be so hard on yourself, David. We're all children inside. Bill evoked a childlike love from you, as well as an adult love." He thumbed through the pages of the book. "Ah, here it is."

Taking his seat, Greg flattened the cover of the opened book onto the desk blotter. "I have an anonymous prose poem here that has proven a great comfort to me, and doubtless to generations of pet owners. It's called Rainbow Bridge. Would you like to read it?"

Not trusting himself, David asked Greg if he wouldn't mind reading it.

The counselor's brows contracted. "Frankly, I was hoping you would read it. I'm not sure if I can get through this, myself. It's a killer. But," he cleared his throat, "here goes. Hang on to your hat."

RAINBOW BRIDGE

Just this side of heaven is a place called Rainbow Bridge.

When an animal dies that has been especially close to someone here, that pet goes to Rainbow Bridge. There are meadows and hills for all of our special friends so they can run and play together. There is plenty of food, water and sunshine, and our friends are warm and comfortable.

All the animals that had been ill and old are restored to health and vigor. Those who were hurt or maimed are made whole and strong again, just as we remember them in our dreams of days and times gone by. The animals are happy and content, except for one small thing; they each miss someone very special to them, who had to be left behind.

They all run and play together, but the day comes when one suddenly stops and looks into the distance. His bright eyes are intent. His eager body quivers. Suddenly he begins to run from the group, flying over the green grass, his legs carrying him faster and faster.

You have been spotted, and when you and your special friend finally meet, you cling together in joyous reunion, never to be parted again. The happy kisses rain upon your face; your hands again caress the beloved head, and you look once more into the trusting eyes of your pet, so long gone from your life but never absent from your heart.

Then you cross Rainbow Bridge together....

The psychologist looked up and managed a husky self-deprecatory laugh. "I should have rehearsed this a few times before you came in; maybe then I would have been able to read it without getting choked up."

David could not talk. The image of Bill greeting him once again, in any capacity, caused such sweet pain. The thought, in fact, was too much to bear with any composure; his mind clamped down. "It's a very nice sentiment," he understated.

"I think so," Greg replied.

The older man relit his pipe, and sighed. "We counselors are in the reality-business, always trying to get our clients to accept and deal with the real world. But when Annie passed away, I'd had enough of the real world. 'Reality' was Annie lying there, cold and inert. And I can tell you that even then I knew *that wasn't Annie.* Annie was somewhere else. Whatever had made her an explorer, a comedian, a little tiger waiting around a corner to ambush me — that energy, or spirit, didn't — couldn't — die. It was somewhere else. This poem comforted me because it gave me a kind of wild hope. Maybe it's silly, but it helped. Now, I don't go around telling my associates that I believe in Rainbow Bridge, but I don't mind telling you there's a part of me that wants to believe it. Maybe it's the inner child. Maybe it's irrational and selfish. But there you have it."

David regarded the counselor with a feeling of gratitude. This was not what he had expected from an appointment with a psychologist.

"I don't think," Greg concluded at the end of their session, "that you need to see me again, unless of course you want to. You're not 'overreacting' and you'll begin to feel stronger in awhile. But I do have a suggestion you might want to consider. I know of a support group for grieving pet owners. There are lots of people who feel just as devastated as you are now — and as I felt, after Annie passed away. This group meets twice a month. The attendees change — as people gradually begin to feel better — but the heart and soul of the group remains constant. Her name is Elizabeth Browning, just like the poet. Here's Betty's phone number; just tell her I recommended her to you. I think you'll benefit from a couple of meetings."

CHAPTER FIVE

AS DAVID PARKED IN FRONT of the address he had been given, he hesitated. Elizabeth Browning had sounded nice enough — and normal enough — but his mind continued to create the most outrageous stereotypes of the bereaved pet owners he expected to attend this group therapy session. He imagined little old ladies sharing photographs of their long-lost lap dogs, pampered cats and parakeets.

And the men who attended these sessions? What kind of man would be so distraught at the death of a household pet that he needed group therapy?

With a wry smile, he acknowledged to himself that he was that kind of man.

Elizabeth Browning's energetic telephone voice belied her true age. The appearance of the elderly woman who greeted him at the door did nothing to assuage his fears of being surrounded by a society of little old ladies who missed their pets. She must have been in her late eighties.

But the grand old lady had a twinkle in her eye as she welcomed David. She liked him immediately, simply because he had come. Anyone, she knew, who missed their departed pets to the point where they needed help, had big, big hearts.

"Come in, David. The gang's all here."

The "gang" turned out to be five people in the living room: three rather elderly ladies who shared the taste in clothes of their generation, a balding man in his fifties wearing a short sleeved shirt and tie, and a teenage girl who appeared perfectly at ease in the company of adults. Counting him and Elizabeth, there were seven. David was grateful for the presence of the other man, who introduced himself as Herb.

"David is here because he just lost his best friend, Bill the Bulldog," explained Elizabeth Browning. "I thought maybe he could sit and listen for a bit, to get a feel for the group. We're all friends, who have lost dear pets. And Herb was about to tell us a story about Buster."

Leaning forward, in fact nearly on the edge of his chair, Herb held a manila folder in both hands. David noticed an aerospace logo on the folder, and assumed Herb to be some kind of engineer. "I have some photos here," he said, "if you want to pass them around."

'Buster', David soon saw, had been a parrot!

Noticing the raised eyebrow on the newcomer's face, Herb smiled with understanding. "Surprise you, David?"

"Well, yes, a bit," David smiled in return. "When I heard the name 'Buster,' I imagined a dog — although now that I think of it, I don't know why."

"Buster was the most remarkable bird in the world," Herb explained with pride. "I grew up with him as a child, and inherited him when my parents died. Buster was an African Grey Parrot, and he talked all day. It was the funniest thing, because you never knew what he would say. And remember: he mimicked voices, so very often he would speak in my mother's or father's voice. It wasn't eerie, or anything like that; I loved my parents and with Buster in the house it was kind of like still having them in my life."

Herb laughed. "He would even resurrect old conversations my parents had, speaking in their voices. Things like (in my mother's voice) 'Are you hungry?' My dad's voice would answer, 'What have you got?' And then Buster would go off on a tangent, repeating 'What have you got?' another thirty times.

"African Greys can live fifty years on average, and have been known to live many years beyond that. So Buster was in my life most of my life. He was the sweetest bird, gentle as can be. Smart, too. And he had a sense of humor. He wanted to be included in all family discussions, and would look at my wife's face, then at mine, as we talked, as if he were following the conversation. He would watch television, as if he were really following the story line. Then he would come out with some hilarious non sequitur and we'd both collapse with laughter. My wife loved him as much as I.

"Buster died six months ago. He must have been all of sixty years old; and the house seems so empty without him."

The teenager, Becky, slowly nodded her head in somber agreement.

"My house seems empty, too. But, in my case, it's my fault.

"Everyone here knows that my Babs was hit by a car," she explained to David. "She was a house cat ninety percent of the time, but I would take her into the garden occasionally. One day I got into an argument with my boyfriend over the phone and forgot that Babs was in the backyard. Well, she must have chased after a bird or something and got out.

"After I hung up the phone, I went upstairs for a long hot, relaxing bath. When I came down, I called for Babs and she wasn't there. Then I thought 'Oh my God, she's still in the backyard! But she wasn't! I searched all over for her, and even began preparing Lost Cat signs for the neighborhood."

Becky lowered her head. "Babs finally came home two days later, barely walking. I could see that she was hurt on one side and rushed her to the animal hospital. That's where she died. And it's all my fault," she insisted with her head up and her eyes brimming with tears.

"Not at all, dear," said Elizabeth, coming over to sit by her side. "Even the most pampered, protected house cat has a hunter streak in them. We have to accept that trait, as we love them. Cats have to explore — and prowl around like little tigers. Babs wouldn't have been happy as a prisoner, forever locked up in the house."

Elizabeth put her arm around the girl's shoulder and turned to David with a warm smile. "So this is what we do here, David. We talk about our departed pets; we share stories and laugh at their funny adventures; and we also cry. And what we discover in these meetings is that we're not alone: there are others who feel the same despair, the same sense of irreparable loss — and sometimes the same sense of guilt."

"I have something to share," volunteered one of the ladies. "It's a letter to my Amy. I lost her," she confided to David, "nearly a year ago to feline leukemia."

Seeing the accepting looks on the other faces in the room, David suddenly felt trapped.

This very normal-appearing little old lady, by the name of Winnie, was about to read aloud her letter to her dead cat, and no one batted an eye.

"This may strike you as odd," interposed Elizabeth in an

understanding voice, "but you may find this — exercise — to be very useful. It may help to think of this 'letter' as an entry in a diary."

Flushing with embarrassment at having been so transparent, David assured her of his interest in the proceedings.

"Well, then," said Winnie as she put on the reading glasses which had been dangling from her neck, "this is it. 'Dear Amy....'"

David, in an effort to look composed, listened politely. But he soon got over the absurdity of the situation by concentrating on Winnie. He could tell by her writing style, and by the articulate manner of her speech, that she was an accomplished woman. Her clothes, he noticed, were really quite impeccable. The way she sat in the chair was relaxed and yet somehow authoritative. He found himself wondering what she had done in her life, and could easily picture her in a leadership position.

Yes, it was true that she was reading a letter to a dead cat; but there no longer seemed anything terribly odd about it. Her sincerity conferred a kind of legitimacy to the exercise — if, indeed, it was an exercise to Winnie. It could have been a letter to her daughter, or to a close friend. And, David began to realize, it was.

As she read, he couldn't help composing the beginning words of a letter of his own....

Winnie concluded her letter to Amy with "Until we met again at Rainbow Bridge."

"My dear Winnie," murmured the lady next to her, whose name was Rose.

"We believe in Rainbow Bridge, you see," a bright-eyed Winnie explained to David. "It helped me deal with my loss at first, but then — the more I thought about it — the more real Rainbow Bridge became to me."

"And why not?" asked Herb. "I'm an engineer," he explained to David. "I deal with facts and figures, and I appreciate Einstein's theory of the conservation of energy. Basically he showed us that energy cannot be destroyed. The energy that made up our loved ones — and I include our pets when I say 'loved ones' — doesn't simply vanish when they die, because energy cannot be destroyed. It follows, then, that the energy must still exist somewhere in a different form, or maybe on a different plane. That's why I don't think the idea of Rainbow Bridge is farfetched at all. Sure, it makes me happy to contemplate the possibility of seeing Buster again, with the rest of my loved ones. But that doesn't necessarily mean that Rainbow Bridge is simply an imaginary self-help tool; it could be a real place."

"I feel it is," testified Rose. "I think love is immortal. I haven't stopped loving my little Dachshund, Foxy, and I don't think she has stopped loving me. It's that simple."

"I'm afraid we're hitting David with a lot at his first meeting with us," said Elizabeth Browning with a smile. "I think you'll find, David, that talking about your Bill, and sharing stories about him, may help you recreate the joy he gave you. Right now you're focused on the loss; but when you let him live again in your mind, despite the sweet pain, you'll begin to focus on the gain — and there was great gain in your life thanks to Bill. By talking about him, you may find that your sorrow begins to be replaced with gratitude for having been so fortunate to have had Bill in your life.

"Now, today," continued Elizabeth, "you just may want to listen to the rest of us talk about our pets. We certainly don't want to put pressure on you. But if you'd like to share a story about Bill, please do. And," she reassured him, "don't worry if you start to cry; we all have, and we'll probably end up crying with you."

"I can vouch for that," said Herb with a sad smile. "I was a basket case when Buster died."

"A funny story about Bill might be easier," suggested Becky with wisdom beyond her years.

David leaned back in his chair and crossed his legs, forcing his body to relax. He took a couple of deep breaths, and began.

"Well, we brought Bill home from the breeder when he was about three months old, maybe a little less. I don't know if anyone here has ever seen a Bulldog puppy, but they're the cutest things in the world. When you saw Bill's face, your heart melted, you just had to kiss him. He still had the sleepy look of a puppy, but he was waking up quickly. When I took him to a vaccination clinic, I stood in line holding Bill. As I approached the table, two of the busy female vets took one look at him and stopped everything. They rose from the table and took him from my arms, kissed his face and fussed over him as if he were a baby. He was the most beautiful puppy I had ever seen — precisely because he was kind of "ugly", as all Bulldogs are. But at this point, that's all he was to me. I had no idea of the kind of personality Bill would develop. He became the most wonderful character — full of humor, incredible energy, courage (if a little afraid at the same time) and surprises, always surprises.

"The first hint he gave me that he had a will of his own was during this puppy period. I would take him for a good walk, and when he'd start to pant, let him cool down on the lawn before I took him inside. Then I would say "OK, let's go in." But one morning Bill looked at me with a mischievous glint in his eyes. He braced himself on the grass, as if to say 'Come and get me.' So, just to see what would happen, I raised my voice a little, repeating the 'command' to come inside. Bill lowered his head and wagged his stubby tail so hard that his whole rump wagged. He suddenly burst off into a tight circle at astonishing speed for a Bulldog, then stopped dead in his tracks and looked at me, daring me to try to catch him. So of course I was totally drawn into the play and I would make a show of trying to catch him, as he buzzed around. Finally, exhausted, Bill flopped over and lay there panting, his eyes animated and happy, watching me. I realized then, that he was playing with me, instead of the reverse."

Elizabeth, appearing quite pleased with David being so forthcoming at his first meeting, exclaimed, "What a little character!"

"Was he a good watchdog?" asked Herb. "My Buster was as good as a house burglar alarm system. He let us know if anyone was at the front door before the doorbell rang. And sometimes, when my wife and I were returning from a dinner out, Buster would challenge us as we approached the door, demanding to know — in my own voice — 'Who's there?'"

David nodded his head in the affirmative. "Bill was so kindhearted that he was not exactly as ferocious as he looked. But there was a time or two when he was a good watchdog. For one thing, his bark wasn't like other dogs; the sound didn't come from the mouth; it emanated from his abdomen; it was more like a roar from the belly of the beast. We heard that roar one night, when somebody tried to break in through our garage door. I went downstairs, a little scared myself, and praised Bill for being such a good watchdog. Then we both headed for the kitchen door to the garage. By now Bill was barking and ready for action. I knew that, with all the noise, the garage was empty at that point, the would-be thief long gone. But I wanted to see what Bill would do. So I opened the door and said 'Go get him, Bill!' But Bill, despite all his huffing and puffing, wasn't about to enter that garage. He peered into the darkness, and then looked up at me, as if to say 'Are you kidding?' He would not budge an inch, no matter how I encouraged him. Once I turned on the light, and walked in myself, demonstrating that the bad guy had left, Bill stormed into the garage and took possession, growling like a lion. It was the funniest thing. But I didn't want to laugh, because I was trying to make a watchdog out of him."

Encouraged, David continued to tell another story about Bill. And as he did, he found himself smiling. This was, in fact, the first time he had smiled when talking about Bill since his death. All his recent thoughts and memories of Bill had produced so much pain, that he had actually been repressing them. He had even gotten into the habit of diverting his eyes from Bill's living room photo; it simply hurt too much to see that happy, foolish, dignified, Bulldog face.

David was smiling, he realized, because he felt that Bill was somehow nearer. It was as if that wonderful personality had been recalled, through the power of storytelling, to his rightful place in David's heart, rather than remaining locked up in saddened memory. He found himself thinking, even as he spoke to the group, "Bill was by nature a bringer of joy; memories of him should not bring pain."

By consensus, the support meetings were scheduled to last no longer than one and a half hours. Buoyed by his experience, David thanked the group and said he would very much like to return.

"Bring pictures of Bill next time, won't you," pleaded Becky. "He sounds so cute."

As he was bidding goodbye to Elizabeth, David suddenly realized that she had not spoken about her own experiences — perhaps because she felt a responsibility as facilitator. That was when he first noticed, on the end table, a small framed photograph of a Pug. The big expressive eyes appealed up to him.

"Elizabeth, is this your story?" he asked.

"Yes," she answered with a sad smile. "That was my little baby. For fourteen years she enriched my life. I've talked about her a lot in these meetings, but we generally defer to the newer members and make sure they've had a good opportunity to express themselves. So today you were spared my stories," she laughed.

"She's very cute. Of course, it's natural for me to like Pugs because they remind me so much of miniature Bulldogs. What was her name?"

Elizabeth's eyes seemed to rejoice at the pronunciation of her pet's name: "Willow."

Chapter Six

RAINBOW BRIDGE held unique experiences for Bill. He had never played with a cat before and, in fact, had kept a respectful distance from cats his whole life. Only once, as a puppy, had he tried to play with a cat — and that had gone fine until Bill had unwittingly cornered the little thing. Ever since that unpleasant experience, Bill had contented himself with issuing a growl upon encountering a cat; but he knew better than to give chase.

Here, however, cats and dogs were no longer adversaries — and were, in fact, playmates. And Bill had made a friend of one. Actually it was Annie who picked him out. The older cat had one day been inexplicably drawn to the massive Bulldog. Bill, now wholly accustomed to the fact that everyone at Rainbow Bridge was eager to play, was nonetheless a little wary at first.

Annie soon dispelled Bill's notion that cats were unreliable, and unpredictable, playmates. He delighted in playing with her because, unlike a dog, which is very open in its desire to romp and race, Annie generally came upon Bill unannounced. Their very first meeting was typical. Bill had been on his way toward his group of friends — Linda, Max, Willow and Rex — when he heard a predatory cry and suddenly felt four paws pouncing on his back! Even though he knew intuitively that no harm could ever come to him at Rainbow Bridge, he was startled. The furry little tiger had ambushed him from a nearby fern.

Annie allowed herself to slide off of Bill's great shoulders and to go to ground. Lying on her back, she held onto Bill's forepaws with her own, while playfully digging at his belly with her soft hind feet. Solid as a monument, Bill looked down into the strange, unreadable cat's-eyes, and then gave out with a throaty Bulldog bellow. Unimpressed, Annie continued to gently paw Bill's tummy, and responded with a meow of her own.

They soon became fast friends and could be seen chasing each other throughout the park. They often napped together. Bill's snores and Annie's purring combined into a kind of duet that

The inseparable trio: Bill, Annie, and Willow.

provided much amusement to the other dogs and cats at Rainbow Bridge.

Willow the Pug also soon became a closer companion. Although she had always admired the Bulldog, she too felt recently drawn to Bill, of all the dogs at Rainbow Bridge. And the three — Annie, Willow and Bill — soon became inseparable.

Chapter Seven

Dear Bill,

One of the ladies in the support group writes letters to her cat, so I can't exactly let the cats get all the letters, now can I?

It's been nearly two months now, Bill, and I still expect you at the door when I come from work.

I miss you and love you so much!

God I wish there was something I could do for you, to make you sigh with contentment. Nothing pleased me more than watching you snore away, happy and safe, and enjoying every aspect of your life. In fact, I don't know what was more fun for me: watching you play to near exhaustion, or watching you flake out afterwards, on your back usually, with your big, reliable chest rising and falling, and that look on your face of happy exhaustion. You made me enjoy my life so much more.

Bill, I'm beginning to believe you are alive in some way — maybe even more alive now than ever. If so, I know you're happy and safe and full of energy.

Oh, how I want to see my Bill again, and to be part of his life forever.

I love you Bill. I see your face — so comical, yet so earnest and sincere — those laughing eyes demanding attention from me. Then I see the expression of contentment while you are receiving that attention. And then I see your querying face, after I paused for a second or two in petting you, as if you were telling me to get back on the job.

Do you remember how you acted whenever I would return from a week-long business trip? Most dogs would jump for joy as soon as their master opened the

door. But not you! While my wife was kissing me, and welcoming me back home, you would get up and actually leave the room. And I could see that you were mad at me for having left you for a whole week! It was so funny, and so touching. So I would follow you into the other room, and sit down beside you on the carpet and talk to you. Finally, after I had placated your hurt feelings, you would turn to me with half-closed eyes and walk up my chest, pinning me to the ground. You would lower your face to mine while I laughed — and you would lick my face all over.

What a nut you were.

I love you, Bill, and miss you so much.

— David

Chapter Eight

BILL HAD MADE A NEW FRIEND at Rainbow Bridge — an Australian Sheepdog by the name of Outback. In fact, Bill was the first one to meet Outback, who had appeared on the horizon as Bill was sauntering through the park in his classic, rolling Bulldog gait.

Outback appeared to have the same reaction to Rainbow Bridge as Bill had, on entering the park. His eyes — one blue, one grey — seemed to delight in the green expanse, where numerous dogs chased each other, and romped and wrestled down the grassy knolls. Bill introduced himself by way of lowering himself into the Bulldog crouch, exposing a lower tooth, and wagging his stubby tail.

Outback, who had never seen an English Bulldog in his whole long life, stood still for a moment as if assessing the situation. Then, seeing the comical light in Bill's eyes, he barked in recognition of a potential playmate. Grey in the muzzle, and recently severely arthritic, the sheepdog soon discovered he could fly like the wind again, and easily dart in and out of Bill's charges. He barked with joy at each new revelation of physical ability; he was himself again, the fastest sheepdog in all of Queensland, and this bulky Bulldog chasing him didn't stand a chance!

Except suddenly Bill spun on a dime and intercepted the quicker dog with his massive shoulder, sending Outback tumbling along the grass and barking with delight. The two became instant buddies. Bill escorted him back to the center of the park, where they both were soon mobbed by Willow, Chi Chi, Rex, Linda and Max. Outback's startling two-colored eyes caused the other dogs to cock their heads in amazement.

Having no sheep to herd, Outback tried to organize Bill, Willow, Chi Chi, Rex, Linda and Max into some kind of directional group. Their answer to his instinctive urge was to mob him with slurping lips and wagging tales until the Australian Sheepdog finally gave up, and joined the group as a playmate, rather than a herder.

One day, as he napped in the shade of his favorite tree, Bill heard a distant bark that he knew well. From the distant reaches of the park, Rex came running!

As the German Shepherd drew nearer, Bill had to marvel at the beauty of the breed. Maybe Rex hadn't been fortunate enough to have been born an English Bulldog, but he certainly made up for that deficiency with his bold gait, magnificent head, and intelligent eyes. Those eyes were now lit with expectation. The normally composed old warrior was almost beside himself with uncontainable happiness.

Bill looked to his right: a human silhouette had appeared on the rise of the hill. Soon Bill could see that it was a man, walking toward the footbridge. With a frantic bark of farewell, Rex flew by Bill and raced toward the man. Eager to see what would happen, Bill followed at a respectful distance. As he drew nearer, he could see the man clearly, and liked what he saw. Like Rex, he seemed to be an old warrior, himself, fearless and composed.

Until he saw the German Shepherd racing toward him.

The tough looking man fell to his knees and shouted out "Rex!"

And the former police dog, who had been trained to "take down" the largest of adversaries, now threw himself onto the chest and shoulders of his former partner, pinning him with his giant paws and licking his laughing face. The reunited comrades tumbled over each other, the man crying out "Rex, Rex!" while the dog barked with delight. Then, just as Zack had done, Rex seemed to take charge of the situation: he walked out onto the center of the bridge and barked, wagging his tail, waiting for his friend to follow.

The man appeared less of a warrior now; the need for being hard and tough had vanished. He seemed at peace with himself. It was as if the lines of care had been smoothed away by Rex's happy licks. He looked more youthful, and expectant. With a broad smile, he followed his trusty comrade across the bridge.

Bill stood at his respectful distance, his stubby tail wagging as he watched the two disappear into the colors of the rainbow.

And, as before, he returned to the play area of the park with a confident glow in his great Bulldog chest.

Chapter Nine

AT THE NEXT group session, David found Greg Baxter sitting on Elizabeth's sofa, grinning up at him. "Betty told me you had come — and how much they enjoyed your stories about Bill. I attend these sessions whenever I can;" he added, "they're good for me."

David was happy to have the substantial, beaming presence of Greg in the room. He would bet the psychologist was dying to light his pipe in Elizabeth's pristine living room, but didn't dare ask.

"This evening," began a tired-looking Elizabeth, "Greg is going to give us an update on the animal rescue facilities he helps support."

"That's right," confirmed the psychologist, with an abundance of nervous energy David felt sure was due to pipe tobacco withdrawal. "As you may know, I became pretty active in animal rescue right after Annie passed away — especially cat rescue. It made me feel as if I was doing something Annie would have approved of," he smiled. "And I have good news to share."

Opening his laptop, Greg went into a brief fiscal report of the three rescue organizations he served, each of which seemed to be garnering a fair amount of community support.

"Now that I've gone over the numbers," he concluded, "let me show you some of the faces of our guests. I've got a little slide show here that you may find interesting."

One by one, the faces of the rescued animals appeared on the computer screen. Not surprisingly, Greg began with the cats. "Many of these lost souls," he explained, "were feral, and in pretty bad shape when we brought them in." It was such a pity, thought David, to see creatures that were made for being loved and stroked — and made for returning love — shrink back and glare at the camera with beautiful, wild, frightened eyes. It seemed incredible that they could be so afraid of the very people who wanted to hold them, caress them, and care for them.

When Greg got to the dogs, David noticed that a number were either Pit Bulls or had a lot of Pit Bull in them. Although they had gentle names, like Alice, Baby Blue and Lover, they were nonetheless Pit Bulls, and David couldn't help thinking they would be hard to place in loving homes. But there were also a few lap dogs that made the ladies utter expressions of sympathy. And even a red Parrot that caused Herb to sit up in his chair! But the bird, Greg informed him, had badly bitten the finger of the owner's wife.

"Some rescued pets have personality issues," confided Greg, "especially if they've been abused. People who adopt some of these pets are a bit like volunteer foster parents to delinquents; they're doing the Lord's work, but it is work."

Continuing with the slide show, Greg added nonchalantly, "And then you have some well-behaved house pets whose owners, for whatever reason, can no longer care for them. Like this old girl...."

Suddenly the earnest face of an English Bulldog appeared on the screen! David's heart leapt momentarily at the familiar features of the breed: the furrowed brow, the pink interior of the little ears, the flat nose, the calm, thoughtful eyes.

Without so much as a glance in David's direction, the psychologist paused. "Roxie, here, is a ten year old female English Bulldog — and she's got all the issues every Bulldog develops sooner or later: skin problems, dry eye, and, of course," he added with a grin, "flatulence. But I've met her and she's a sweetheart, I can tell you that. Kind, gentle — and very much her own person."

As Greg moved on to highlight other "guests" of the rescue facility, the image of the old Bulldog lingered in David's sight. The thought of getting another dog hadn't seriously occurred to him; it had in fact seemed blasphemous — an act of disloyalty to Bill, who could never be replaced. And yet Roxie was looking for a home. She was a Bulldog in need, and a female — so there could be no question of her replacing Bill.

Perhaps by doing a favor for the breed in general, he would be pleasing Bill.

David carried on this internal argument well into the group session, as each member shared another story of their departed pet. Greg Baxter had left for an appointment, but not before casting a concerned glance at Elizabeth, who looked quite wan. As he took his leave, he dropped a few of his business cards on the table, "in case anyone wants to meet one of our rescued guests."

One by one, the group members shared warm and loving memories of their departed pets. When David's turn came, he spoke with a fond smile.

"One of the really strange and funny things about Bill was his love for high places. As a puppy, he would climb up everything he could. For example, he would work his way up the dining room chairs to the top of the table, and just stand there as if he were claiming a mountain peak in his name. Once he climbed up the open drawers of the kitchen cabinets onto the kitchen counter. Another time, my wife and I returned from a dinner out to find Bill asleep on our stove top! How he got there, we couldn't figure out; neither of us saw a convenient route to the top.

"Now, that was one habit of Bill's that I really had to discourage. As an adult, he weighed 70 pounds And, because of his massive shoulders, most of that weight was forward. He could have easily broken a foreleg jumping down from these heights. And there were times when I would come home and find him limping. Fortunately, that was a habit he eventually grew out of.

"Bill was such a character," continued David. "Sometimes I would round the corner into the living room and find Bill rounding the corner, himself. We would both stop in our tracks, confronting each other. I wouldn't say anything for a moment; Bill would remain motionless, a monument of muscle, his earnest eyes looking up at me.

"I'd ask, 'Is there anything wrong?'

"He'd give me a low, playful growl.

"I'd back up a step, pretending to be frightened, and ask 'Do you have rabies?'

"Bill would then bark in the affirmative.

"Then I'd back up another fearful step and say 'Oh my God, he's got rabies!' and Bill would charge at me, head down, and ram himself into my legs. I'd pretend to fall down and we'd wrestle, with me yelling 'Oh no, a rabid dog,' and Bill growling and barking like a movie stunt dog."

David found himself grinning at the memory.

"Bill liked to be near me. I'd be reading in the den, and Bill would sleep by my side. I'd get up, and he would open one eye, watching my movements. I'd go into the living room and, before long, Bill —

now fairly certain that I wasn't returning to the den — would ramble in and resume his nap next to me, lying on his side and snoring. It was very complimentary to have that big, solid dog follow me around.

"But, if the truth were to be known, I followed him around, too. I'd always look for him, and then make a point of going over and petting him. I probably stroked him with hundreds of strokes every day, played with his ears, and scratched his furrowed forehead. He'd sit there, his massive back turned to me, as if he couldn't care less. But the instant I'd stop, he would look back at me as if to say 'Why did you stop?' When I resumed the petting, he'd turn away again, like a client getting a massage at a health spa."

The members of the group each had kind comments to make. David felt happy to be in the room with such sympathetic souls. He decided, then and there, to remain in the support group even after the pain of losing Bill had subsided; maybe he could help others going through what he was going through now.

As they all took their leave, with hugs and smiles, David again noted that Elizabeth appeared to be ill.

"You'll have to excuse me, David; I'm not quite myself today."

"There's flu going around," he ventured, "maybe you have a touch of it."

"I'm sure that's all it is," she sighed.

Chapter Ten

DAVID AND SUSAN JACKSON arrived at the rescue facility at their appointed time. Greg Baxter had apparently briefed the volunteer manager of David's recent loss.

"So you're a Bulldog lover?" he grinned as they shook hands.

"Yes, we're very fond of the breed," David replied in forced nonchalance.

The manager led the way to the dog area — or tried to lead the way. But Susan, her maternal instincts aroused, was drawn to virtually every warm and fuzzy pet in the place. Every kitten, and every puppy, pulled at her heartstrings.

She wanted to adopt them all.

The manager, accustomed to such responses, patiently introduced the couple to virtually each pet. Reading Susan accurately, he kept away from the reptile terrariums.

But David's eyes were on the elderly female English Bulldog long before they arrived at her little living space.

Roxie was not a "cute" Bulldog. Many Bulldogs, like Bill, are so "ugly" they're cute. But Roxie, poor thing, did not make that transition; she remained ugly. Her lower jaw thrust forward by an extra half inch, by breed standards; her eyes were cloudy with age; and one of her ears had an obvious yeast infection. Her left forepaw turned in, as if it had been broken and then healed at an unnatural angle — so that, when she walked, she appeared crippled. She drooled, even though the facility was air-conditioned. Upon closer inspection, Susan commented that she smelled like a wet blanket.

Nonetheless, David's senses rejoiced at the sight and feel of an English Bulldog. For all her faults, she was a Bulldog. He was, in fact, relieved that her condition was so unlike Bill's; there was no basis for "competition" with the heroic legacy of Bill. Roxie was a wreck.

But, as he soon discovered, a lovable wreck.

She had an engaging way of rolling over — "Like a pig in the mud," Susan dryly observed — for her belly to be rubbed. And she had an almost coquettish way of reaching out with her maimed forepaw to poke at David whenever he stopped scratching her tummy.

It was clear to David that Roxie made a poor comparison with the other younger and healthier rescued dogs, and that she might be the last one adopted — if adopted at all. Even Susan seemed dubious. David felt sure that she would have chosen another dog for the house, and he wouldn't have blamed her at all.

But his wife was, in actuality, thinking of David first. She worried about him; and if this creature would help him come out of his depression, she would make the best of it.

"Honey," she heard herself saying, "if Roxie will make you happier, let's bring her home."

That night, David wrote another letter.

Hi Handsome,

We brought an old dog home today, Bill. You'd like her, I think, even though she'd never have been able to

keep up with you.

Her name is Roxie. She's got a lot of health problems and probably not much time left. But she is an English Bulldog, and when I look into her eyes I see fleeting glimpses of you.

When I look at her, my heart leaps suddenly because she has all your features; then my heart breaks because she isn't you. That's unfair to Roxie, of course; she can't help it if she isn't you.

We'll give Roxie a home for the rest of her life, because it's very possible that no one else would. But she'll never replace my Bill. She never could. No dog could or ever will. When you were alive, I never looked at another dog. Now that you're gone, I don't need to — not after having Bill the Bulldog in my life.

His thoughts were interrupted by the appearance of a worried-looking Susan.

"Honey, there's a very sad message on the answering machine from Greg Baxter. It's about Elizabeth Browning."

Chapter Eleven

AT RAINBOW BRIDGE, Bill, Willow and Annie could be seen together almost all the time. Although they enthusiastically played with each and every newcomer, and with the older residents, they always seemed to end up with each other.

Annie was generally the inventor — or, more properly, the instigator — of each new game. Bill's reaction was to launch himself into every suggested activity, and Willow would follow suit, eager to please the big Bulldog and the clever Tabby cat.

One afternoon, after a particularly fun romp through the park, they all lay happily down together and prepared to nap.

Suddenly, they heard a distant human voice!

Elizabeth Browning arrives at Rainbow Bridge.

"Willow....Come Here, Sweetie.....Willow....Come Willow."

During Bill's time at Rainbow Bridge, he had never heard a pet actually summoned by the call of a human voice. But there could be no doubt of it: the far-off voice called for their friend — who now, no longer tired, sat bolt upright on the alert.

All three looked toward the source of the voice and, sure enough, a human figure could be seen walking down the hill toward the distant footbridge. Bill could discern that it was an older woman; but her stride was confident, and her voice, sweet and strong. She had not seen them yet, as she searched the park with her eyes.

Willow, after a startled look at Bill and Annie with her big expressive eyes, took off running as fast as her little legs would carry her.

Elizabeth Browning spotted the movement and stopped. She knelt in the grass and opened her arms, awaiting the barking, squealing Willow, who in her eagerness, had tumbled more than once, falling forward into a ball and resuming her race toward the woman she had loved her whole life.

Tears of joy and confirmation streamed down Elizabeth's cheeks. Rainbow Bridge existed! She had been right to believe in her reunion with Willow!

From their respectful distance, Bill and Annie watched the two eventually — after much joyful petting and hugging — venture upon the footbridge. For the first time in Bill's experience at Rainbow Bridge, the human did not have to be beckoned and led by the pet. In fact, she crossed the bridge with Willow in her arms. Bill could see that she strode confidently forward, her face radiant with the colors of the rainbow. Willow, carried like a baby, looked trustfully, with her big round eyes, up into the beloved face of her greatest friend.

When the couple had disappeared into the colors of the rainbow, Annie seemed lost in thought. Bill wondered if it was the cat's first time at witnessing the great miracle of Rainbow Bridge. She looked at Bill and meowed tentatively, as if confused. Then, all of a sudden, she seemed to grasp the implications of what she had just witnessed — and completely lost her cat-like composure.

Annie was so happy, in fact, that she leapt on Bill and hung onto his neck, meowing and purring with the joy of understanding. Carrying her on his great shoulders, Bill trotted back to the center of the park, his body rolling in the classic Bulldog gait.

Chapter Twelve

Dear Bill,

Last night, or rather, in the early morning hours (probably about the same time in the morning that you died) I had a dream that felt like a gift from God. I was walking you, trying to hold you back because, as usual, you were charging forward. In the dream I knew you would soon be tired; but, again as usual, you couldn't help yourself from going full bore.

I dropped the leash and lunged forward, grabbing your sides. I rolled you over on your back and patted your belly, thinking, "This dog is in top shape, but he's got a little Bulldog pot, and it's so damn cute." Then, in the dream I began to realize — as I rolled you upright, and kissed the top of your head — that this was a special moment.

Someone was talking to me; it was the sweet voice of woman. Perhaps it was the voice of Elizabeth, but I can't remember. The voice said, "Bill has come back to visit you, but he can only stay a short time. I'm going to leave you two alone, now." And then suddenly you were on your back again, growling the way you used to growl when you played with me, and I was rubbing and tickling your chest, and your eyes were looking directly into mine, and they were so full of play and joy that I woke up bursting with happiness, myself, my heart pounding in my chest. And I said over and over again, "Thank you, God, for this dream."

It was so real. And it was so wonderful to have you back again. I've never had anybody bring such pure joy into my life, and I felt that joy all over again.

I may read this, years from now, and think I must have been a nutcase at the time of this writing. But the deal

I made with myself, when I started writing these letters, was to censor nothing, and to put down what I'm feeling.

Ah, but I am a lucky man to have had you as my closest pal! Of all the people who have lived on earth, only I had you — the greatest Bulldog of them all.

You lived a full, fun life and I will not shy away from enjoying my memories of my best friend. So, if I have to, I'll make myself face the pain and move through it and think about you all I want, without sorrow.

Oh my pal, I'm so lucky to have had you in my life — the one and only Bill. The one and only Bill! I only hope you were lucky to have me.

— David

ON A SUNNY MORNING, David took Roxie to the park — Bill's park — his heart still heavy from the day before. A special service for Elizabeth Browning had been held, at Greg Baxter's suggestion, at a pet memorial park. Some two hundred people had come, many held pets in their arms; many stood in the circle and expressed their gratitude for that wonderful, giving lady.

David had never been to a pet cemetery before. At some time he had seen a brief news clip of a police burial ceremony for a heroic police dog killed in action — and had been very moved by the honor and respect paid to the German Shepherd. It was clear that the police officers in dress blues considered the Shepherd a fallen comrade. But, other than that, he had never visited a pet cemetery and had hardly been aware of their existence.

At its entrance stood the graceful image of St. Francis of Assisi, the patron saint of animals, surrounded by statues of entranced little creatures. Beyond lay a peaceful garden with wrought iron benches; and, beyond that, little headstones marked with names like "King," "Bowser," and "Trixy" dotted the property. As he walked through the park after the memorial service, David discovered that many of the little monuments had "hearts" and short poems painted on them.

No; he certainly wasn't alone in his grief over the loss of a pet.

On his way back to the car, he passed again the statue of St. Francis, and had a fleeting, sentimental image of the patron saint of animals personally welcoming Elizabeth Browning in heaven. At that point, tears had filled his eyes.

And now, he watched Roxie make her way over to the bushes in the park where he had spent countless happy hours with Bill. There was no question of hurling the soccer ball for her to chase down, or of wrestling with her. Passersby would not gaze in admiration at her, and the soccer players might wonder what ever happened to that remarkable Bulldog who could handle a ball with the best of them.

But Roxie touched his heart in different ways. Although crippled, she was determined; although nearly blind, she explored the world around her methodically. She was not the embodiment of spontaneous joy Bill had been, but rather a patient, plodding survivor of life — perhaps a harsh life. And he wanted to make her remaining years as pleasant as possible. He felt he was doing it not only for her, but for the breed, and for Bill.

Roxie emerged from her foray into the bushes and searched about for David with her clouded eyes. "Here I am, old girl." When Roxie turned her head toward him, she appeared to David — who could read Bulldogs rather well — grateful for his presence, and for his protection. Once satisfied of his nearness, she ambled off to explore another part of the park, which was still very new to her.

David watched her patient progress and realized that he was becoming quite fond of Roxie — in a different way, surely, but quite fond. She was a sweetheart.

And, he also realized, it was OK. He felt that Bill would have approved and, in fact, did approve. Bill had been joy incarnate — a transient being that wished for and expected happiness whichever way he turned. He would have wanted David to be happy — and especially happy in this park, where they had played together for so many years.

David let out a sigh of relief.

It was as if he had been given permission to love again.

His eyes took in the broad expanse of the green park, where Bill had once ruled. He imagined Bill rushing at him, with that wacky, out of control happiness that was so vulnerable, like the spontaneous delight of a child. He recalled how he would drop to his knees to wrestle Bill, and how Bill would charge. He would get

David and Roxie at the park.

a last glimpse of Bill's funny face before he ducked for cover and felt his hot breath on the back of the neck, and felt the tickle of his "ferocious" growls.

To have had that gift from God.... "That's what Bill was," he thought, "he was almost like an angel, here on Earth. He represented, in the midst of life with all of its stresses, the possibility of pure, unadulterated joy.

"I wasn't his master, at all," David realized, "Bill was *my* guardian; he may have felt a responsibility to cheer the human up, to make him smile back."

Goosebumps appeared on David's arms. "Bill had a soul," he said aloud. "And, if the soul cannot be harmed, or destroyed, it still lives."

The image of the pet memorial park came again to him. He recalled some of the names of the pets painted on the little tombstones. And suddenly, involuntarily, he imagined the souls of the buried pets scampering above ground — animated with an energy that was eternal — romping and playing on the grass as they were meant to, instead of lying insentient beneath the earth.

It was simply not possible that Bill's incredible exuberance could be quelled by the mere circumstance of death. He had loved Bill; Bill had loved him. Love, also, was immortal. Elizabeth Browning had realized this. And that was why she felt confident in the existence of Rainbow Bridge, where beloved pets were the transitional guides to the afterlife.

As David walked slowly behind the plodding, snuffling Roxie, his mind began to piece things together. According to the laws of nature, he could only have had Bill under his care for a comparatively short time. Those years had passed. But they had passed consciously. He had never taken Bill for granted; he had never put him in the background of his busy life. He had taken very good care of Bill and had, in fact, been one of the reasons behind Bill's transcendent happiness. And he felt inexpressively grateful for the opportunity to have buoyed Bill's spirit, just as Bill had buoyed his.

Elizabeth Browning had, he now decided, been reunited with her Willow. And he, too, would see Bill again at Rainbow Bridge. He felt it; he knew it. And the certainty of once again witnessing Bill's love of life filled his heart with gratitude and with joyful anticipation.

David looked at his watch. His wife would have made breakfast by now. It was Sunday, and that was something she enjoyed doing.

He realized he was hungry.

"Come on, Roxie, old girl," he called cheerfully. "Let's go home."

Epilogue

AT RAINBOW BRIDGE, Bill had finally figured out a way to catch Annie at her own game. While an English Bulldog is not a particularly stealthy dog, Bill knew how to hide. He found that by breathing through his mouth, and not snuffling — and controlling his stubby tail — he could make himself very hard to find among the ferns near Annie's favorite tree. There Bill would wait, with his dancing eyes, for Annie to saunter by.

It turned out that Annie, for all of the fabled awareness of cats, was not above being ambushed, herself.

And when Bill pounced, he pounced! Annie found herself possessed by a powerful grip of forelegs. Bill would growl into

Annie's ear, which made the cat struggle and meow with feigned indignation. When she managed to escape (always wondering if Bill simply released her) Annie would dive head first into Bill's great, big, soft chest and hang on for dear life. When Bill rolled onto his back, Annie was carried along — and the two would growl and meow, and have a great time playing on the soft green grass.

At the end of a long play session, the cat and dog would invariably snuggle together for a profound nap. Bill liked to have Annie nearby; her purring relaxed him. For her part, Annie appreciated the deep, comforting snore of the Bulldog.

With Annie almost asleep, purring on his big chest, Bill cast a sleepy look on the great, green expanse of Rainbow Bridge. Dogs and cats everywhere played with each other. Colorful birds conversed in the branches, and flew majestically through the air, without fear.

As Bill turned his honest face toward the white puffy clouds dotting the blue sky of Rainbow Bridge, he could sense the presence of an abiding love. Just as he had felt during his whole lifetime, Bill felt loved and protected by a powerful and benign guardianship.

Although he wasn't physically tired, Bill looked forward to his

Bill and Annie nap at Rainbow Bridge.

nap, and to the wonderful sense of peace that always followed his dreams of his friend, David, the person he had loved most of all.

As he began to doze off into a deep Bulldog nap, Bill took in one last panoramic glance of the endless park at Rainbow Bridge. What a wonderful place! How lucky he was! And how lucky he had been to have known and to have loved his friend, David.

Bill's trusting eyes scanned the top of the hill, where the human figures would occasionally appear to the delight of their beloved pets.

It was not his and David's time yet; but he knew deep in his big heart that he, too — like Zack, Rex and Willow — would eventually be reunited with his loved one. Then he and David would, like all the others, cross the footbridge together into the dazzling colors at the end of the rainbow.

Bill's great chest sighed with pleasure at the very thought of it. And the memories of David that usually came to him only in dreams now warmed his big Bulldog heart in the full light of day.

Utterly content and confident, Bill closed his sleepy eyes. After his nap, he would play with Annie; and they would romp with the other dogs and cats at Rainbow Bridge, where all the pets are always happy all of the time.

THE END